Maths

KINGFISHER

First published 2010 by Kingfisher
an imprint of Macmillan Children's Books
a division of Macmillan Publishers Limited
20 New Wharf Road, London N1 9RR
Basingstoke and Oxford
Associated companies throughout the world
www.panmacmillan.com

ISBN 978-0-7534-1965-6

Consultant: Dr Troy P Regis

Designed and created by Basher
www.basherbooks.com
www.basherworld.com
www.bebo.com/simonbasher

Dedicated to David Coleman

Text and design copyright © Toucan Books Ltd 2010
Based on an original concept by Toucan Books Ltd
Illustrations copyright © Simon Basher 2010

9 8 7 6 5 4 3 2 1
1TR/0410/UNT/SHENS/128MA/C

A CIP catalogue record for this book is available from the British Library.

Printed in Taiwan

Note to readers: the website addresses listed above are correct at
the time of going to print. However, due to the ever-changing nature
of the internet, website addresses and content can change. Websites
can contain links that are unsuitable for children. The publisher cannot
be held responsible for changes in website addresses or content, or
for information obtained through a third party. We strongly advise
that internet searches should be supervised by an adult.

CONTENTS

Chapter 1

Counting is one of the easiest things. One, two, three, four. And with ten handy counters at the end of your arms, getting to ten doesn't take much brainache. But what are the Number Bunch for? Well, they're essential if you want to do sums. They work in lots of tens. Ten tens becomes one hundred, ten hundreds becomes one thousand and so on. So far so good, but maths has a bad habit of getting harder. The Number Bunch are here to stop things becoming befuddling and boring. When it comes to crunching numbers, they're the ones that count!

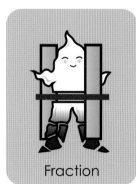

Zero

Infinity

Minus Numbers

Fraction

Decimal Fraction

Units

Zero

▥ Number Bunch

- ✹ Youngster who has two lives, as a digit and as a number
- ✹ This digit allows you to imagine huge and teeny numbers
- ✹ It's also a tricky, mysterious number that equals nothing

I am El Zero, and I can dissolve you to nothing. You know my sign, the round mark of Zero. So be warned! I have extraordinary powers. Pop my digit at the end of a number and I make the number ten times larger – leaping from 1 to 10 to 100 to 1000 and so on forever. And then there's the curse of Zero. Divide by me and your calculator will return a big fat ERROR! Multiply by me and any number – no matter how large – vanishes, reduced to… well, Zero.

You see, I am something that stands for nothing. I am called nix, zip, zilch, nada, zippo… Hovering between being and not-being, I am one of the most important numbers in maths. Yet I am so strange, so puzzling, that for hundreds of years even the cleverest European mathematicians didn't understand or use me.

Indian mathematicians first used Zero as a number 2500 years ago.

- ● First book to include Zero: written 628CE
- ● Came to Europe via Muslim scholars
- ● The number Zero is an even number

Zero

Infinity

▦ Number Bunch

- ✴ A mindboggling customer that lies beyond all limits
- ✴ You cannot count or measure to Infinity or ever reach it
- ✴ Not a number, but closely involved with numbers

You'll never pin me down. I'm Infinity, beyond what you can even begin to imagine. Inconceivable! OK, start counting: 1, 2, 3, 4, 5, 6... And keep on counting: 7, 8, 9, 10, 11, 12... And then count some more, and some more and some more. Hey, you say, this could go on forever. That's just the point! I exist, sure enough, and yet you will never reach me. I'm that endless road that teasingly keeps on disappearing off into the unknown.

Actually, I have a confession to make. Shh! Don't tell the others. I'm *not* a number – you can't use me to add or multiply or do the other things you do with numbers. But I'm so tied up with them all that I feel fine about being here. By the way, my symbol is written like this: ∞. It's a closed double loop, rather like a figure 8 taking a nap.

Georg Cantor (1845–1918) spent his life studying Infinity... and went mad!

- ● Symbol name: lemniscate
- ● Symbol introduced by: John Wallis (1655)
- ● Medieval symbol: snake biting its tail

Infinity

Minus Numbers

▦ Number Bunch

- ✴ These minusy-guts allow us to count lower than Zero
- ✴ A Minus Number is the inverse (opposite) of a positive one
- ✴ These negative numbers turn Add and Subtract on their heads

We are the beasts who live under the stairs. Count backwards on the number scale: 7, 6, 5, 4, 3, 2, 1. It's like blast-off, isn't it? Then you reach the dark guardian of the gate, Zero. After that, you're with us, my friend, lurking in the dusty depths: –1, –2, –3, –4, –5, –6, –7…

We're the opposites of the numbers you use to count real-life objects, such as apples, sweets or your dad's grey hairs. Here, in the magical world of maths, strange things happen. In the everyday world, you can't Subtract more than you have. You can't take nine biscuits from a tin that has only five biscuits in it, can you? But with us at your side, nothing could be easier. You're left with Minus Four biscuits. Minus Four is the inverse of number four. If you add four to Minus Four, you get Zero.

Used to describe things like freezing temperatures, eg –23 °C.

- ● First known use: China (3rd century BCE)
- ● First used by Arabs: 1000CE
- ● First used by Europeans: 17th century

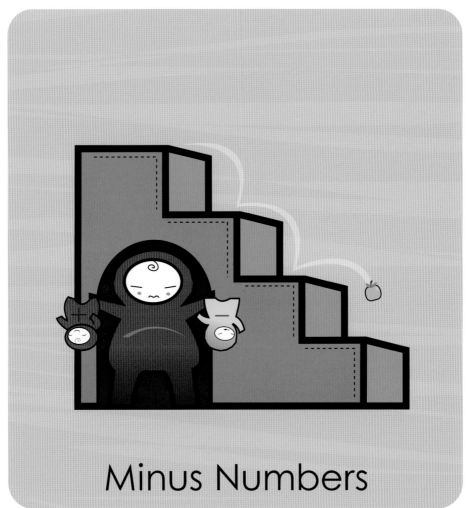

Minus Numbers

Fraction
Number Bunch

* Shadowy figures lurking in the gaps between whole numbers
* Fractions are used to count the parts of a whole
* The top figure is the numerator, the bottom the denominator

We're the broken bits and pieces. You can count whole pies on your fingers, but what if someone cuts a pie into four equal parts and eats a slice? That's where we come in – not-quite-whole numbers. We look like this: $1/4$, or $2/3$ or even $1/600$. The bottom bit says how many parts the whole is broken into – four in the case of $1/4$. The top says how many of those pieces you have – one.

Fraction

Fractions are used in shops to give discounts, such as $1/2$ price.

● First known use: China (c.2800BCE)
● Proper Fractions: less than one (eg $5/7$)
● Improper Fractions: more than one (eg $9/7$)

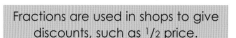

Decimal Fraction

Number Bunch

* The same as Fractions, but shown a different way
* Written as a figure or figures following a dot, or decimal point
* Points mark the end of whole numbers (147.5, 14.75, 1.475)

Decimal
Fraction

OK, so we're smart and orderly! Got a problem with that? Here's an example of our skills: 0.25. Scruffy old Fraction would call it $1/4$. To get from Fraction to us, use your calculator to divide Fraction's top bit by the bottom bit. But we're not always tidy clever clogs. Fraction's $1/3$ – one divided by three – becomes our 0.33333333. The threes recur (go on) into Infinity.

● First used by Arabs: 10th century CE
● Digits on left of point: whole numbers
● Digits on right of point: Decimal Fractions

In some countries, people use a comma (,) for the decimal point.

Units

▥ Number Bunch

- ✹ There is a world to measure and this lot do the measuring
- ✹ Divvy up all sorts, such as: length, weight, temperature, time
- ✹ Their main co-workers are things like rulers and stopwatches

We are crack teams, highly trained, orderly and ready for action. Our mission? To sort out the number world's measuring problems. How long is a football pitch? Call in our specialist metre Unit. How much lemonade is there in that bottle? The litre squad are the guys for you. How heavy's the cat? Hurrah! Here comes the gram brigade. Anything you can measure, we've got the measure of it.

We come in all sizes. Take the metre crew. If it's ladybirds or ants you're measuring, millimetres (mm for short) are what you need. For creepy-crawly spiders, centimetres (cm) may be best. Metres (m) are for larger pests, such as your big brother. Usually, these form neat blocks of tens and thousands: 10 mm = 1 cm, 1000 mm = 1 m. But time divides into Units of 60 and 24! Go figure!

The International System of Units (SI) is based on the French metric system.

- ● Number of seconds in a minute: 60
- ● Number of minutes in an hour: 60
- ● Number of hours in a day: 24

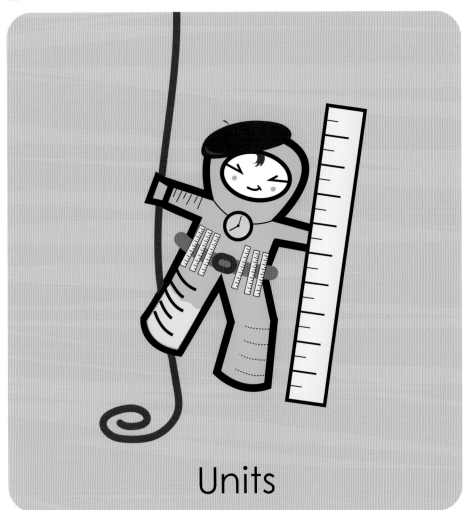

Units

Chapter 2
▪ Special Sum-Things

You'll find this gang of number-crunchers wherever you go. Get the hang of them and you're well into cracking the mysteries of numbers. The Special Sum-Things are ways of combining numbers, finding differences between them, sharing them out and zipping up and down the number scale with ease. They are mostly mental – not bonkers – and just the sort of trick that you can do in your head. Using them can get you out of a tight spot. They will stick with you through thick and thin, and with them on your side ain't nobody gonna make a fool outta you!

Add

Subtract

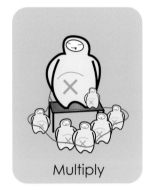

Multiply

Divide

χ

+ Add

■ Special Sum-Things

* With its big plus sign, this little fella joins numbers together
* The work it does is called "addition"
* In maths, the total added up is called the "sum"

Out of all the Special Sum-Things, I'm the one who gives you more. Because I like putting bits and pieces together, numbers usually get bigger with me (the exception is when you Add a Minus Number to a positive number and get a smaller number: 3 + (–1) = 2, for example!).

I'm really simple to use – to Add numbers together, just stack one on top of another and count up each column separately, from right to left. You can use a calculator, an abacus or your fingers and toes. And with me, you don't even have to do things in an orderly fashion: 27 + 35 + 8 is the same as 35 + 8 + 27, which is the same as 8 + 35 + 27. They all Add up to 70. The only number that foxes me is Zero, because he makes no difference to any of my totals. Tally ho!

HEAD PUZZLE You've got 12 red sweets and 18 blue sweets. How many have you got in total? Try breaking the numbers up a bit. 10 + 10 = 20. Right? That's easy to do in your head. And 2 + 8 = 10. So it's 20 + 10, which equals 30. Hurrah!

Add

— Subtract
Special Sum-Things

- ⚹ This unhappy character breaks numbers apart
- ⚹ The work it does is called "subtraction"
- ⚹ The total left over after subtraction is the "difference"

People think that I'm an old misery guts. OK, I admit it, I'm the exact opposite of Add, that bubbly ball of smirking positivity. Because I'm always taking things away, numbers tend to get smaller with me around (the only exception is when you Subtract a bigger Minus Number from a smaller Minus Number and get a positive number: $(-3) - (-5) = 2$!).

I have my uses, though, and some people like me. Ask any cupcake craver, fudge fiend or jelly-bean junky. With my long-dash minus sign, I'm their favourite, because the only way to enjoy cake is to Subtract a slice. But if you want your piece of cake, you have to mind your manners – I demand order. As you know, 5 pieces of cake minus 2 pieces is not the same as 2 pieces of cake minus 5 pieces (which is impossible in real life but possible in mathematics!)

> **HEAD PUZZLE** You buy a bag of 49 fruit chews. Sally nicks 14. How many have you got left? Try counting on. 14 to 20 is 6. Easy-peasy! 20 to 40 is 20. And then there's the last 9. $6 + 20 + 9 = 35$. So $49 - 14 = 35$. Get it?

Subtract

✕ Multiply
■ Special Sum-Things

- ✸ A greedy guts who hoards numbers together
- ✸ This big guy's work is called "multiplication"
- ✸ In maths, the total provided by multiplication is the "product"

When I'm around, whole numbers get much bigger, much faster than with that tiresome Add. This is because I gather up whole groups of numbers rather than just single units. Three times four means three helpings of four, which gives you much more than three plus four (12 rather than 7, if you must know). My sign is x, the sign of the times! Memorize your times tables and I'll make you rich.

I do have one thing in common with Add – neither of us is fussed about order. Two lots of number 3 is the same as three lots of number 2. The number 1 cramps my style a bit. Multiply any number by 1 and you get the same old number you started with – one lot of number 11 is plain and simple 11. As for Zero… use me to Multiply by Zero, and you get nothing. Zero lots of number 5 is always zilch-o.

HEAD PUZZLE Tom gives you a bunch of four marigolds. All marigolds have 13 petals. How many petals are there in the bunch? Well, 4 = 2 x 2, so the bunch has 2 x 2 x 13 petals. That's better! 2 x 2 x 13 = 2 x 26 = 52.

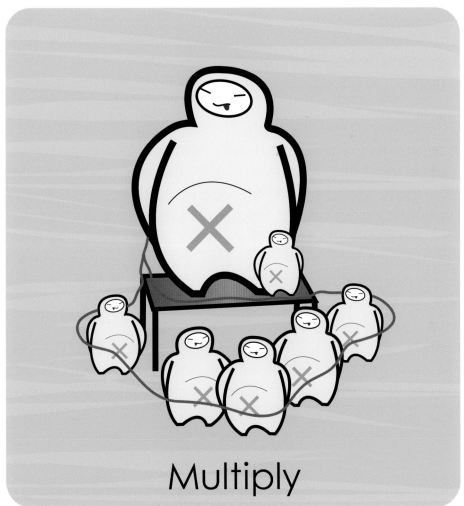

Multiply

÷ Divide
■ Special Sum-Things

- ☀ An equal-minded pirate who portions out numbers fairly
- ☀ This even-steven's work is called "division"
- ☀ In maths, the number being divvied-up is called the "dividend"

I'm Multiply's opposite, here to share out the loot and make sure everyone gets even portions of the pie. If there's one of you, you can have the stash all to yourself, but if there's more than one, you need me. You'll find me an even-handed sort of fella, one who always does the carving up fairly. But one thing's for sure – dividing by a whole number makes the total number go down. In other words, each portion I give is smaller than the total amount. You have to use Multiply to get back to where you started.

Sometimes, I can't split things up into neat round numbers. So, in my quest for fairness, I use underworld connections and create Fractions – shady, not-quite-whole-numbers who make the sum work. My sign is ÷, the division sign, which also has the fancy Greek name "obelus".

> **HEAD PUZZLE** You, Jane and Andy are going to buy a toy that costs £12.21. How much does each of you have to chip in? Hey! That's why you learn your times tables. 3 x 4 = 12. Yes? And 3 x 7 = 21. So each owes £4 and 7p. Or £4.07.

Divide

χ

■ Special Sum-Things

✳ A nameless secret agent who haunts maths equations
✳ This "χ"-citing creature has been operating for over 1800 years
✳ Used in algebra to help you work out unknown quantities

I am the faceless one. With my secret codename "χ", I lurk in the shadows of the Special Sum-Things gang. I am what's called a variable – a mark put in place of an unknown, mystery quantity. I am "χ"-tremely useful and not just to friendly old mathematicians.

Let me "χ"-plain. Say that you and Angus buy a bag of sweets. You both eat two sweets and Angus hides four more in his pocket. If you bought 10 sweets, how many are left in the pick-and-mix bag? 2 sweets + 2 sweets + 4 sweets + x (unknown amount of sweets left in the bag) = 10. With me to help, you don't have to look in the bag. Instead, work it out on your fingers that $x = 2$. Argh! That means Angus nicked most of the goodies! See? I've the x-factor! Goodness me, all this punning is "χ"-hausting!

HEAD PUZZLE Keep calm! Think straight! Your marbles have scattered all over the place. Amy's found 11. Pete's found 8. You had 24 in all. OK, 11 + 8 + x (the number missing) = 24. 11 + 8 = 19. Take that from 24. You've still got 5 to find.

χ

Chapter 3
Shape-Shifters

Slippery! Slidy! These are the Shape-Shifters, the building blocks of everything you see around you. Maths has them and their shifty ways down to a fine art – it's called geometry. Where two straight Lines meet, you get an Angle. Three straight Lines and three Angles make a Triangle. This is magic! A square has length and width, right? Both the same. Give it depth as well and it can become a cube. In the world of geometrical shapes, you move through dimensions, from 1D to 2D to 3D. This is the best building set you'll ever have. Enjoy!

 Line

 Angle

 Circle

 Pi

 Triangle

 Quadrilaterals

 Polygon

 3D Shapes

 Area

 Volume

Line
▦ Shape-Shifters

- ✳ A simple character who lives in 1D only
- ✳ In geometry, a Line has length but no width
- ✳ Lines are said to intersect when they meet or cross one another

I'm the simplest shape there is. Think of me as the skinniest beanpole you ever came across. Just length in 1D – that's all. A Line that's neither 2D nor 3D. The other Shape-Shifters look down on me for my uncluttered lifestyle, but let me tell you one thing: not one of them can be drawn without me.

When I take the shortest route between two points – as the crow flies – I'm a straight Line. When I curve elegantly, I'm an arc. And here's another fact – I'm infinite. When you see a Line with two ends, it's only a part (or segment) of me. Sometimes I intersect with another Line, forming an Angle. Sometimes I run parallel with another Line. So, like train tracks, my parallel Line and I never move away from each other and we never move any closer.

Greek mathematician Euclid wrote about Lines and geometry, c.300BCE.

- ● Perpendicular Lines cross at right Angles
- ● Parallel Lines always run side by side
- ● Chord: a Line linking two points on a Circle

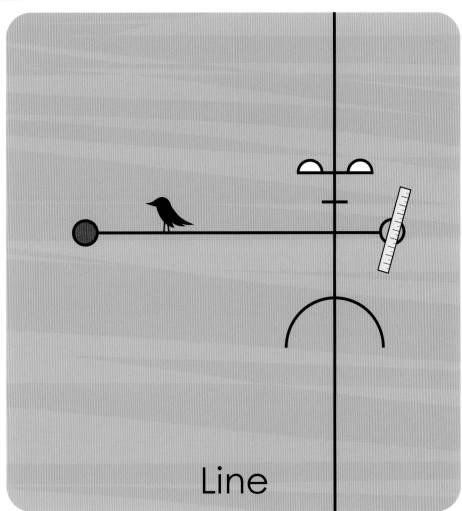

Line

Angle
▥ Shape-Shifters

✳ A sharp customer, found where two Lines meet
✳ Measured using degrees, often written as a small circle: 60°
✳ You use a protractor to measure Angles

No angel, I'm a big cheese face who has many moods. Sometimes I'm just right. Other times, I can be acute, obtuse or reflex. OK, down to business. Imagine two straight Lines on a page. Unless they're parallel, their paths will cross and that's where you'll meet me. If you imagine turning one of the Lines so that it sits snugly on top of the other, I'm the amount you have to crank it around.

If you're a skateboarder, we're already mates. Mastered the 360? Well, 360 is short for 360° – a full or whole turn. What about a neat quarter turn? That's 90°. A 90° Angle is a right Angle – right, proper and exact. Acute Angles are less than 90° – sharp and not so sweet. Then you get the obtuse Angles that blunder along between 90° and 180°. Any Angle bigger than 180° is a reflex Angle.

In geometry, Angles are shown by a small arc between two Lines.

● Whole turn (Circle): 360°
● Half turn (straight Line): 180°
● Quarter turn (right Angle): 90°

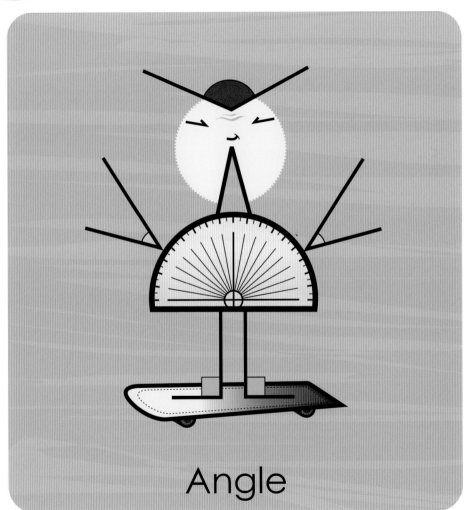

Angle

Circle
Shape-Shifters

* Perfectly rounded, this character is a real roller
* All parts of its edge are the same distance from its centre
* You need compasses to draw a perfectly round Circle

I'm a chubby-cheeked bundle of fun. Every time you draw a happy face, chances are it's beaming out of me. And of course any time you hop on your bike and pedal down the road or do a wheelie, you're using my cool talent for spinning, or rotating. Yes, I get things rolling. It's a knack I owe to one simple fact – all points on my perimeter (the outside line that forms my shape) are an equal distance from my centre.

I'm so one-of-a-kind that my vital statistics have their own special names. My width is called my diameter (d). The distance from my centre to my perimeter is my radius (r) – half my diameter. The length of my perimeter is that noble fella, circumference (C) – "Sir Cumference". To measure my Area (A), you'll need the help of my friend Pi (π).

In ancient times, many people believed that the Circle was divine.

* Diameter: $d = 2 \times r$
* Circumference: $C = \pi \times d$
* Area: $A = \pi \times r \times r$

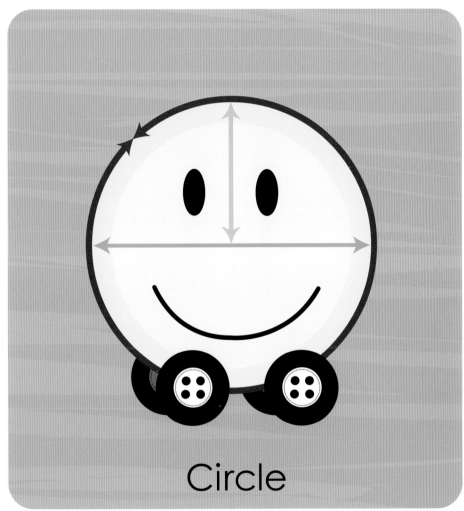

Circle

π Pi

▪ Shape-Shifters

- ☀ A mysterious number with many maths tricks up its sleeve
- ☀ Defined as the Ratio of a Circle's circumference to its diameter
- ☀ Often written as the Greek letter π, pronounced "pie"

As simple as Pi? Hmm! Up to a point. Mathematicians love me – I'm their favourite dish (pie, geddit?). But I take a bit of getting used to. How do you find me? Take Circle's circumference and Divide that by the diameter. It doesn't matter how large or small the Circle is, the number you get will always be the same – me, Pi!

Crazy, isn't it? And they do call me an irrational number, which could mean that I'm gone in the head. But I'm sane, really. It's just that you can't capture me neatly in a Fraction. So what is my magic number? 3.14159… and on and on and on. The number never ends and never repeats. Spooky! And don't think I'm just some funny little oddity. No, I'm key. For example, you need me to work out the Area of a Circle. And that's just one of my tricks.

Pi to 20 decimal places:
3.14159265358979323846

- ● $\pi = C \div d$
- ● π: first letter of Greek word for perimeter
- ● Surface Area of a sphere: $4 \times \pi \times r \times r$

Pi

Triangle
Shape-Shifters

* Three corners and three straight sides – that's a Triangle
* There are four different kinds of Triangle
* A Triangle's three interior (inside) Angles add up to 180°

"Tri" pushing me around, big fella, and I'll knock you into a three-cornered hat. I'm rigid! Three means strength, and you'll need a sledgehammer to shift my shape. I do have different forms, though. Come meet them!

Prettiest first! Meet the equilaterals – all three sides the same length, with three dainty 60° Angles. Next, the isosceles – two sides the same, two equal Angles. Uh oh! Here come the scalenes – no sides or Angles the same. Last, the right-Angled Triangles, with one 90° corner. These dudes hook up with a famous rule, Pythagoras' Theorem: "The squaw on the hippopotamus equals the sum of the squaws on the other two hides"... Just kidding! "The square of the hypotenuse equals the sum of the squares of the other two sides."

If "c" stands for hypotenuse, Pythagoras' equation is $a^2 + b^2 = c^2$.

* Area: $1/2$ x length of base x height
* Right-Angled's longest side: hypotenuse
* Right-Angled's other sides: legs or catheti

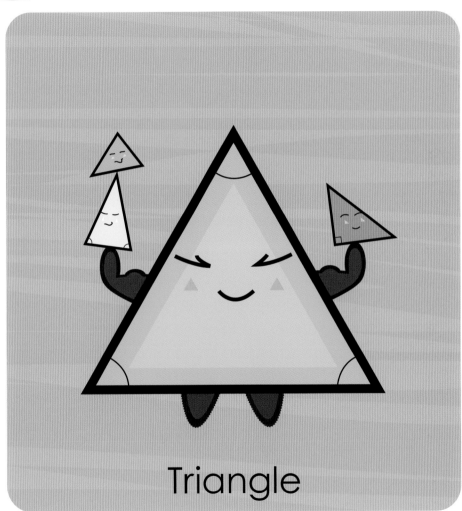

Triangle

Quadrilaterals

▥ Shape-Shifters

* ✵ These boxy squaddies all have four straight sides
* ✵ They include squares, rectangles and many more
* ✵ The name comes from Latin words meaning "four sides"

Sharp-edged and orderly, we march to a strict rule of four – four corners, four straight sides. Squares are special Quads, neatly turned out with four 90° Angles at their corners and four equal sides. But don't think we're just a load of old squares – we come in all sorts of shapes.

Rectangles let two of their sides grow longer but keep their corners at a 90° Angle. Rhombuses (like wonky squares) and parallelograms (like wonky rectangles) live life on the slant. They let their corners slide off the right Angle, although their two pairs of opposite sides are still parallel. Tricksy trapeziums only bother to keep one pair of parallel sides, while kites (shaped like the ones you fly) have no parallel sides at all. Kites, though, are symmetrical – one half mirrors the other.

The geometrical kite was named after the shape of flying kites.

* ● All Quadrilaterals have: 4 sides
* ● All Quadrilaterals have: 4 corners
* ● Interior Angles: add up to 360°

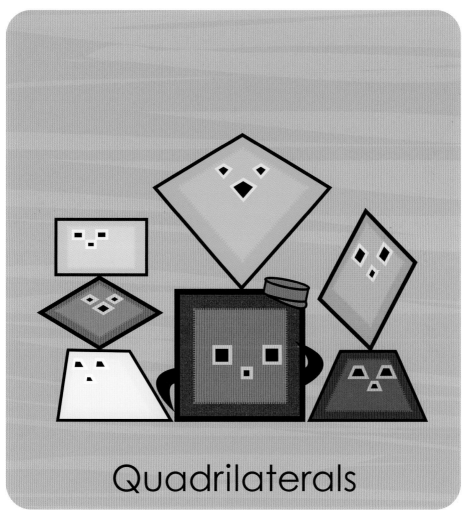

Quadrilaterals

Polygon
▦ Shape-Shifters

- ✳ The right royal ruler of the 2D flatlands
- ✳ Includes all geometrical shapes with straight sides
- ✳ The name comes from Greek words meaning "many Angles"

I'm the queen of diamonds (the four-sided ones in packs of cards) and many more. But before I start boasting about my loyal subjects, let's count to ten in Greek – don't worry, I know what I'm doing. Here goes: *ena* (one), *dio* (two), *tria* (three), *tessera* (four), *pente* (five), *hexi* (six), *hepta* (seven), *octo* (eight), *ennea* (nine), *deca* (ten).

Excellent! Well, you've already met my trusty Triangles (*tria*, three, see?) and my worthy Quadrilaterals. Here are some of the others: my pentagons (five-sided shapes), hexagons (six-sided), heptagons (seven-sided), octagons (eight-sided) and so on. Some are regular, with equal sides and Angles. Some are highly irregular – their sides a jumble of lengths, their corners a ragbag of Angles. But they are all mine, all Polygons.

A Polygon with a million sides is called a megagon.

- ● Enneagon (or nonagon): nine sides
- ● Decagon: ten sides
- ● Hendecagon: eleven sides

Polygon

3D Shapes
Shape-Shifters

* The 3D top dogs of the Shape-Shifter gang
* They live in the same 3D world we all live in
* 3D Shapes have depth (or height), as well as length and width

We're space cadets. We fill space. Think of that poor Line, with length but no width or depth. Or even the Polygon crew with length and width, but still no depth. With us, you get all three – length, width and depth. Cubes, spheres, cones and pyramids, that's us – objects you can sit on, store things in or kick around a park.

There's loads that's special about us 3D guys. Each of us fills up a certain space, called its Volume. Our surfaces, like skins stretched over us, have Area. In geometry, each of our sides is called a face. Our faces meet along edges, which come together in pointy corners. Each corner is called a vertex, from an old Latin word meaning "top", like the spiky top of a mountain. Our oddball is the sphere, which has just the one face – no edges and no vertices.

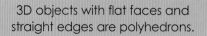
3D objects with flat faces and straight edges are polyhedrons.

* Cube: boxy shape with six square faces
* Sphere: round like a snooker ball
* Cone: round base, pointed tip

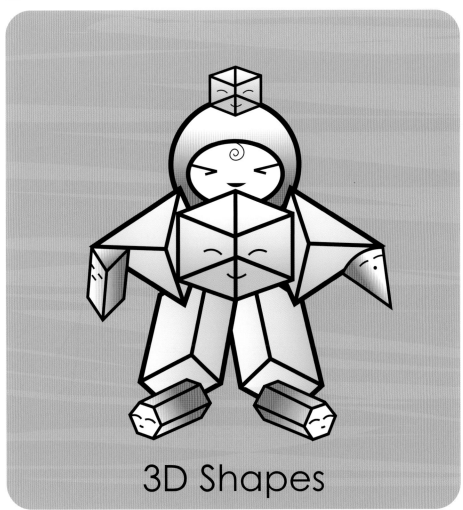

3D Shapes

Area
▦ Shape-Shifters

✳ Nerdy but handy, this character sizes up 2D space
✳ The size of any surface, flat or rounded, is its Area
✳ Measured in square Units, such as square metres (m²)

I'm like a piece of cloth rolled out over something – the top of your kitchen table, for example. The amount of 2D space I cover is the thing's surface Area. Some call me flat and boring, but they're just plain wrong. Every surface has its Area, and that includes the surface of your football. Nobody can call that flat and boring.

Right! Let's get to work. Grab a biscuit tin! How big's the top of the tin? OK, measure how long the top is – 23 cm, say. Then measure how wide it is – 20 cm. Multiply one by the other – 23 x 20 – and that's me: 460. The top of your tin has a surface Area of 460 cm². Easy, wasn't it? You can carry on. Do the same thing with the tin's other five faces, then Add all your results together. You now have the tin's total surface Area – top, bottom, sides and all.

> Land area is often measured using hectares or acres.

● 1 hectare = 10,000 m²
● 1 acre = nearly 4047 m²
● Area of UK: 244,820 km²

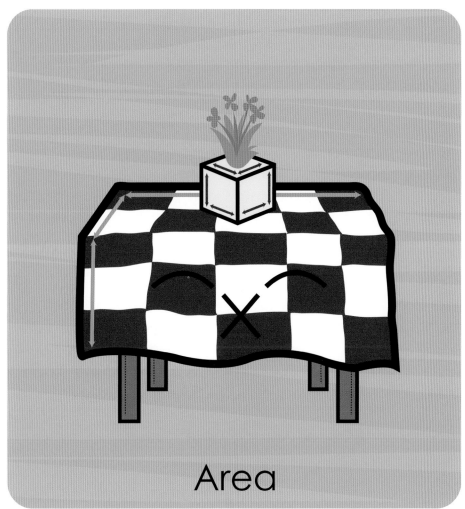

Area

Volume
▥ Shape-Shifters

* ✴ A funky rocker used to measure 3D space
* ✴ The amount of 3D space a thing takes up is its Volume
* ✴ Measured in cubic Units, such as cubic metres (m^3)

"Turn up the Volume, babe." When you think of me, that's what you imagine, isn't it? Loud music and big rock-star hair. Well, I have other skills. I can tell you the size of a 3D object – that kind of Volume. Even better, I work hand in glove with capacity – how much of something another object will hold. Now, that can be truly vital information, like how much fizzy pop a bottle contains.

Remember Area's biscuit tin? It was 23 cm long and 20 cm wide. OK, let's say it was 9 cm deep. What's its Volume? Easy-peasy! Multiply the three numbers together and you get me: 23 x 20 x 9 = 4140 cm^3. For rounded things like bottles, you'll have to get in touch with Pi. Always happy to lend a hand, Pi will help you calculate the Volumes of cylinders, cones, spheres and other curvy 3D Shapes.

Capacity is usually measured
in Units called litres.

* ● Volume of cube: a^3 (a = length)
* ● Volume of cylinder: height (h) x π x r^2
* ● Volume of cone: $^1/_3$ x h x π x r^2

Volume

Chapter 4

Hot stuff, this lot! Data is information – key statistics, like how tall you've grown over the past few months or how many goals your favourite football players have scored. But what's the point of this stuff if you don't do something with it? The Data Gang will show you how. Turn those goals into a kind of picture (or graphic) – a multicoloured Bar Chart, where you can see at a glance who's scored the most. Draw a Line Graph showing how fast you've shot up! Work out some Averages! Calculate percentages! You'll be so busy, you won't know where the time's gone.

Average

Ratio

Per Cent

Bar Chart

Pie Chart

Line Graph

Average
■ Data Gang

* ✹ There's nothing ordinary about this Average Joe
* ✹ Its special skills are finding mid points among numbers
* ✹ Has three forms: the mode, the median and the mean

It's Captain Average to you. My name may be Average, but there is nothing "bog standard" or "plain vanilla" about me. Yes, I drive down the middle of the road so no one can overtake me. But that's my job – working out the exact midway point among a set of two or more numbers.

Take my "mean" trick. Your Aunt Mary – every time you visit her, she gives you a bag of sweets, bless her! Last time, the bag had 19 sweets in it. The time before it had 16 sweets, and the time before that seven. What's the Average (or mean) number of sweets she's given you per visit? Add up the total number of sweets: 19 + 16 + 7 = 42. Divide your total by the number of visits: 42 ÷ 3 = 14. Over three visits, she's given you an Average of 14 sweets per visit. Not bad, really. She's not mean!

The Greek letter μ (mu) is sometimes used for the mean.

* ● Mean: Average of a set of numbers
* ● Mode: most common number in a set
* ● Median: the middle value in a set

Average

Ratio

■ Data Gang

* This tidy person loves to keep things in proportion
* Shows how much there is of one thing compared with another
* Written as numbers with colons between them, such as 4:1

OK, let's cut to the chase! You've got five marbles in your hand, right? Two are red, three are blue. The Ratio of red marbles to blue ones is two to three – that's 2:3. You can also use me for the odds (or chances) of something happening. If you toss a coin, there are two possible results, both equally likely: heads or tails. The odds of getting heads or tails are 1:1.

Ratio

Map scales use Ratio, eg 1:5000 (in life everything is 5000 times bigger).

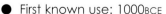

● First known use: 1000BCE
● Ratios can be written as Fractions: 2/3
● Order is important: 5:2 is not 2:5

Per Cent %
Data Gang

* A pin-striped slicker whose name means "per hundred"
* A kind of Fraction, based on parts of a hundred
* Can be written using its special % symbol: 40 %, 75 %, 100 %

Per Cent

I keep track of things, like your score in a quiz. There were 20 questions and – genius that you are – you got 17 right. What's that as a percentage? Divide 17 by 20 and you get 0.85. Multiply that by 100 and you get 85. That is your score: 85 %. Your brother did a quiz with 50 questions and got 38 right. Who did better? Answer: you did – he only got 76 % right.

* 25 % of something is a quarter of it
* 50 % of something is half of it
* 75 % of something is three-quarters

Banks use percentages when people borrow money from them.

Bar Chart

■ Data Gang

* ✳ Smart and brightly coloured, a chart that puts data into bars
* ✳ Good for data to do with frequency – how often, how many
* ✳ Also good for preferences, such as people's favourite bands

In my fancy uniform, I'm off the charts for showing data in graphic (picture-like) form. I'm best when you want to compare things like results. Say that so far this season Fred has scored six goals for the team, Tony's kicked four between the posts and you've scored two. I'll turn that into a chart, where Fred's bar is highest, Tony's is a bit shorter and your bar is the lowest.

Bar Chart

Statistical Bar Charts that display ranges of data are called histograms.

● Invented by: William Playfair (1786)
● Bars can be vertical (upright)
● Bars can be horizontal (left to right)

Pie Chart
Data Gang

* A pie-maker who shares fairly but not equally
* Shows data as Angles within a Circle
* The biggest scorer of anything gets the largest slice

Pie Chart

I offer the tastiest treats if you need wedges of data. When I divide a Circle into different-sized slices – actually, Angles – you'll see at a glance who the big cheeses are. Let's grab those goal results from Bar Chart. Give the tallies to me, and you'll see that out of 12 goals scored so far this season, Fred's scored half, Tony a third and you... well, never mind!

● Pie Charts divide into: segments
● Calculate Fred's Angle: $6/12 \times 360 = 180°$
● Tony's Angle: $4/12 \times 360 = 120°$

The nurse Florence Nightingale used Pie Charts in the 1850s.

Line Graph
■ Data Gang

- ✴ A smooth customer who plays dot-to-dot with data
- ✴ Best for the kind of data that changes over time
- ✴ Has a horizontal x-axis and a vertical y-axis

Plotting and planning, I'm the secret agent of the Data Gang. But when I show you my results, everything's out in the open. My top-notch skill is for things that change over time – like your height during the past six months. First, you'll have to become a plotter like me. Draw your axes – said "ax-eez", not the "ax-iz" you use to chop wood – and label them tidily. The x-axis runs left to right along the bottom and the y-axis runs upwards on the left.

Put time along the x-axis – from 0 to 6 if you're plotting (showing) how much you've grown over six months. The y-axis is for the other set of data – your height. Put a dot or cross for how tall you were at the start of the six months, how tall you were after one month, after two months and so on. Join the dots with lines, and there's your graph.

A pair of numbers called coordinates show a position on a Line Graph.

- ● Coordinates written like this: (2,5)
- ● First number: position on x-axis
- ● Second number: position on y-axis

Line Graph

Index

O

obtuse Angle 32

P

parallel Lines 30
parallelogram 40, 63
pentagon 42
Per Cent (%) **55**
perimeter 34, 36, 63
Pi (π) 34, **36**, 48
Pie Chart **57**
Polygon **42**
polyhedron 44
prime number 64
protractor 32
pyramid 44, 64
Pythagoras' Theorem 38, 64

Q

Quadrilaterals **40**, 42, 63

R

radius 34, 36
Ratio 36, **54**
rectangle 40
reflex Angle 32
rhombus 40
right Angle 32
right-Angled Triangle 38

S

scalene Triangle 38
segment 30, 57
shapes
  1D 28, 30
  2D 28, 30, 34, 38, 40, 42,
    46, 63, 64
  3D Shapes 28, 30, **44**, 48,
    62–64
SI Units 14, 64
sphere 36, 44, 48
square 40
Subtract **20**
symmetry 40, 64

T

trapezium 40
Triangle 28, **38**, 42

UV

Units **14**
vertex 44, 64
Volume 44, **48**

X–Z

χ **26**
x-axis 58, 62
y-axis 58, 62
Zero **6**, 10, 22

Glossary

Abacus A counting frame with horizontal rows of beads.

Algebra A branch of maths that uses symbols and letters to represent unknown amounts.

Arc Part of the circumference of a Circle, or a section of a curving Line.

Average see **Mean**.

Axis (pl. **Axes**) On a graph, the two reference Lines: the horizontal (for the x-coordinate) and the vertical (for the y-coordinate). The axis is also the "mirror image" Line in symmetry – the midway Line that divides a symmetrical object into two halves.

Capacity The amount something can hold. Another word for Volume.

Coordinates A pair of numbers (or letters) that are used to give positions on graphs and maps. They mark the point where a vertical Line on the x-axis meets a horizontal Line on the y-axis.

Difference The amount left over after subtracting one number from another; the difference between two numbers.

Digit A symbol used to make numerals. There are ten digits: 1, 2, 3, 4, 5, 6, 7, 8, 9 and 0. For example, the digits 1, 7 and 4 make the numeral 174.

Divisor Any number that can Divide the number being divided (the "dividend") without leaving a remainder.

Dozen A set of twelve.

Edge A Line where two faces of a 3D Shape meet. For example, a cube has 12 edges.

Estimate A rough calculation.

Even number A number that can be divided by two – even numbers end with 2, 4, 6, 8 or 0.

Face A flat side of a 3D Shape. For example, a cube has six faces.

Formula A mathematical rule written using symbols.

Geometry A branch of maths that deals with shapes.

Inverse A term which means "opposite" in maths: subtraction is the inverse of addition.

Mean The arithmetic average. To calculate the mean, Add up all the amounts in a collection of data and Divide this by the number of amounts: $(50 + 25 + 25 + 45 + 55) \div 5 = 40$.

Median The number in the middle of an ordered set of numbers. If the set is 25, 25, 45, 50 and 55, the median is 45.

Metric system A system of measurement based on multiples of ten (tens, hundreds, thousands etc).

Mode The number that occurs most often in a set of numbers. If the set is 50, 25, 25, 45 and 55, the mode is 25.

Odd number A number that cannot be divided by two – odd numbers end with 1, 3, 5, 7 or 9.

Parallelogram A Quadrilateral with two pairs of equal-length, parallel sides and equal, opposite Angles.

Perimeter The distance around the outside of a 2D shape.

Glossary

Perpendicular Lines that meet each other at right Angles.
Prime number A number that can only be divided by itself and 1, such as 5, 7, 11 and 13. 1 is not a prime number.
Pyramid A 3D Shape with either a triangular base and three triangular faces, or a square base and four triangular faces.
Pythagoras' Theorem Named after the Greek mathematician Pythagoras (c.580BCE–c.500BCE). He came up with a formula to solve the length of a right-Angled Triangle's hypotenuse (the longest side): $a^2 + b^2 = c^2$.
Remainder The amount left over when a number does not Divide evenly.
SI Units The International System of Units is a metric system based around seven defined Units, including: kilogram (weight), metre (length) and second (time).
Sum The result from adding numbers.
Symmetry A property of a 2D or 3D Shape that can be reflected or rotated to "match" or fit with itself in another orientation. For example, the letter "A" has one Line of symmetry and an equilateral Triangle has three.
Transformation To change a shape in one of three ways: flip (reflect), slide (translate) or turn (rotate).
Vertex (pl. **Vertices**) A corner of a 3D Shape. For example, a cube has eight vertices.
Whole number A number that you can count with – somewhere from Zero to Infinity.